Trouble Brewing

A Fun Song About the Boston Tea Party

By Michael Dahl

Illustrated by Brandon Reibeling

Special thanks to our advisers for their expertise:

Tom Mega, Ph.D., Department of History
University of St. Thomas (Minnesota)

Susan Kesselring, M.A., Literacy Educator
Rosemount–Apple Valley–Eagan (Minnesota) School District

PICTURE WINDOW BOOKS
MINNEAPOLIS, MINNESOTA

Managing Editor: Bob Temple
Creative Director: Terri Foley
Editor: Kristin Thoennes Keller
Editorial Adviser: Andrea Cascardi
Copy Editor: Laurie Kahn
Musical arrangement: Elizabeth Temple
Designer: Melissa Voda
Page production: The Design Lab
The illustrations in this book were created digitally.

Picture Window Books

**5115 Excelsior Boulevard
Suite 232
Minneapolis, MN 55416
1-877-845-8392
www.picturewindowbooks.com**

Printed in the United States of America.

Library of Congress Cataloging-in-Publication Data
Dahl, Michael.
Trouble brewing : a fun song about the Boston Tea Party / author, Michael Dahl ;
illustrator, Brandon Reibeling.
p. cm. — (Fun songs)
Summary: Relates the Revolutionary War adventures of colonists who dressed as Mohawk
Indians and dumped tea in Boston Harbor to protest unfair taxes, interspersed with verses
of original song lyrics to be sung to the tune of "My Bonnie Lies Over the Ocean." Includes
bibliographical references (p.) and index.
ISBN 1-4048-0131-6
1. Boston Tea Party, 1773—Juvenile literature. 2. Boston Tea Party, 1773—Songs and music—
Juvenile literature. [1. Boston Tea Party, 1773. 2. United States—History—Revolution,
1775-1783—Causes. 3. Boston Tea Party, 1773—Songs and music. 4. United States—History—
Revolution, 1775-1783—Songs and music.] I. Reibeling, Brandon, ill. II. Title.
E215.7 .D34 2003
973.3'115—dc21   2003009838

SING ONE! SING ALL!

It's the new historical ditty:

"Trouble Brewing."

Sing along to the tune of "My Bonnie Lies Over the Ocean."
Tell the tale of some brave men and boys.
They turned Boston Harbor
into the world's biggest teapot!

Long ago, Americans were called colonists. Their ruler was the King of Great Britain. King George III made the colonists pay money to him. This money was called taxes.

The people didn't think the taxes were fair. Sugar, paper, coffee, paint, and tea were taxed. In 1773, many colonists stopped buying tea. They did this so the king would not get the tea tax. They wanted to show him that they were tired of his way of taxing.

Many colonists wanted to be free of Britain. They called themselves patriots. On December 16, 1773, some of them taught the king a lesson. This song tells the story of that night.

3

Boston

Great Britain lies over the ocean.
Great Britain lies far from our shore.

The king and Great Britain do not fit
in American lives anymore.

The king ruled from far away. He did not travel to America.

Great Britain

5

Give us, oh, give us,
give us our liberty – ber-tee!

Give us, oh, give us,
oh, give us our liberty!

Great Britain sent soldiers and snoopers.
The redcoats were hittin' us hard.

British troops were all over. The patriots called them redcoats. The name matched the troops' bright red jackets.

We were punished, put down, and imprisoned, living our lives under guard.

The soldiers made sure the king's taxes were paid. People who argued were thrown into jail.

11

Give us, oh, give us,
give us our liberty – ber-tee!

Great Britain sent taxes to squeeze us.
The king felt we owed him a fee.

In Boston, we sneaked to the harbor.
We found ships where tea
had been stored.

We opened the locks and the boxes
and dumped all the tea overboard!

Around 50 men and boys disguised themselves as Mohawk Indians. They rowed out to the ships and climbed on board. They tossed all 342 chests of tea into the harbor!

Take back, oh, take back,
take back your crummy old tea, your tea.

And we'll take, oh, we'll take,
oh, we'll take our liberty!

Trouble Brewing

Great Brit-ain lies o-ver the o-cean. Great Brit-ain lies far from our

shore. The king and Great Brit-ain do not fit in A-mer-ic-an

lives an-y-more. Give us, oh, give us, give us our

lib____ er - ty — ber - tee! Give us, oh, give

us, oh, give us our lib____ er - ty!

2. Great Britain sent soldiers and snoopers.
   The redcoats were hittin' us hard.
   We were punished, put down, and imprisoned,
   Living our lives under guard.
   Give us, oh, give us,
   Give us our liberty —ber-tee!
   Give us, oh, give us,
   Oh, give us our liberty!

3. Great Britain sent taxes to squeeze us.
   The king felt we owed him a fee.
   We Americans thought it was unfair
   And decided to stop drinking tea!

   Give us, oh, give us,
   Give us our liberty — ber-tee!
   Give us, oh, give us,
   Oh, give us our liberty!

4. In Boston, we sneaked to the harbor.
   We found ships where tea had been stored.
   We opened the locks and the boxes
   And dumped all the tea overboard!
   Take back, oh, take back,
   Take back your crummy old tea, your tea.
   And we'll take, oh, we'll take,
   Oh, we'll take our liberty!

Did You Know?

Did you know about the boy who climbed out his window to join the Boston Tea Party?
Peter Slater worked for a rope maker in Boston. Peter was only 14 years old. The rope maker did not agree with the patriots. He liked being ruled by the king.

The rope maker heard there would be trouble at the harbor. He knew Peter wanted to be there, too. The rope maker locked the boy in his upstairs bedroom. Peter tied his bedsheets together. He used them to climb down the side of the house. Peter joined the patriots at the harbor.

Peter and his friends taught the king a lesson. They proved to him they would not pay the high tax. After the Boston Tea Party, other colonies started dumping tea, too.

GLOSSARY

harbor—a place where ships dock to load and unload items and passengers

liberty—another word for freedom

patriot—a person who loves and fights for his or her country

tax—money that people pay to their government

tea—a drink made from leaves of a shrub or plant

To Learn More

AT THE LIBRARY

Edwards, Pamela Duncan. *Boston Tea Party*. New York: Putnam, 2001.

Fritz, Jean. *Can't You Make Them Behave, King George?* New York: PaperStar Books, 1996.

Stanley, Diane. *Joining the Boston Tea Party*. New York: HarperCollins, 2001.

ON THE WEB

America's Story from America's Library

http://www.americaslibrary.gov

Offers stories from American history

Boston Tea Party Ship and Museum

http://www.bostonteapartyship.com

Tells the story of the Boston Tea Party and explains the museum

Fact Hound

Fact Hound offers a safe, fun way to find Web sites related to this book. All of the sites on Fact Hound have been researched by our staff.

http://www.facthound.com

1. Visit the Fact Hound home page.
2. Enter a search word related to this book or type in this special code: 1404801316.
3. Click on the FETCH IT button.

Your trusty Fact Hound will fetch the best sites for you!